MW01379331

Sand Dunes

Peggy J. Parks

KIDHAVEN
PRESS™

THOMSON

GALE

San Diego • Detroit • New York • San Francisco • Cleveland
New Haven, Conn. • Waterville, Maine • London • Munich

THOMSON

GALE

© 2004 by KidHaven Press. KidHaven Press is an imprint of Thomson Gale, a part of the Thomson Corporation. Thomson is a trademark and Gale are registered trademarks used herein under license.

KidHaven™ and Thomson Learning™ are trademarks used herein under license.

For more information, contact
KidHaven Press
27500 Drake Rd.
Farmington Hills, MI 48331-3535
Or you can visit our Internet site at http://www.gale.com

LIBRARY OF CONGRESS CATALOGING-IN-PUBLICATION DATA

Parks, Peggy J., 1951–
  Sand Dunes / by Peggy J. Parks.
    p. cm. — (Wonders of the World)
Includes bibliographical references (p.   ).
Summary: Discusses sand dunes including how and where they form, the animals and plants that live in dunes, the dangers dunes pose to people and towns, and the efforts to stop damage caused by shifting dunes.
  ISBN 0-7377-2057-3
  1. Sand Dunes—Juvenile literature. [1. Sand Dunes.] I. Title. II. Series.
  GB632.P27 2004
  551.3'75—dc22
                                                                2003024347

Printed in the United States of America

CONTENTS

Amazing Mountains of Sand

Sand dunes are some of the earth's most beautiful and intriguing natural wonders. They are found on all continents, from the deserts of Africa to the shores of North America's Great Lakes. Some dunes are small, but others tower more than a thousand feet high. They may be shaped like mounds, crescents, ridges, or stars. Yet no matter what size or shape they are, or where they are located, these amazing mountains of sand have fascinated people for centuries.

A Product of Sand and Wind

Although sand dunes exist throughout the world, certain conditions are necessary for them to form. There must be an abundant supply of loose sand as well as enough wind to blow the sand into piles. Usually dunes begin to form where there is an obstacle to stop the sand from moving, such as a bush, a piece of driftwood, or a rock. Cliffs and mountains can also serve as barriers that stop sand and allow it to collect. The sand continues to pile up in a drift that grows larger and larger until a dune is formed. With enough time, and enough sand, even the tiniest anthill has the potential to grow into an enormous dune.

One thing that differentiates dunes throughout the world is the type of sand they are made of. Sand is composed

Sand dunes are formed when the wind blows loose sand into huge piles.

of tiny particles of minerals and rocks that were once part of larger rocks and mountains. Most dunes throughout the world are made of sand that is largely quartz crystals, but there are other types of sand as well. For example, the White Sands dunes in New Mexico are almost entirely made of gypsum sand. These dunes are both unusual and stunning because of their brilliant white color—so white they look like they are mountains of snow rather than sand. On the island of Hawaii, a very different type of dune can be found. Sand composed largely of volcanic lava particles has been swept by the wind into dunes that are glistening black.

Nature's Glass

Just as sand dunes are formed by wind, they can also be affected by another of nature's elements: lightning. It is very

The immense heat of a lightning strike can cause grains of sand to melt into hollow tubes of glass called fulgurites.

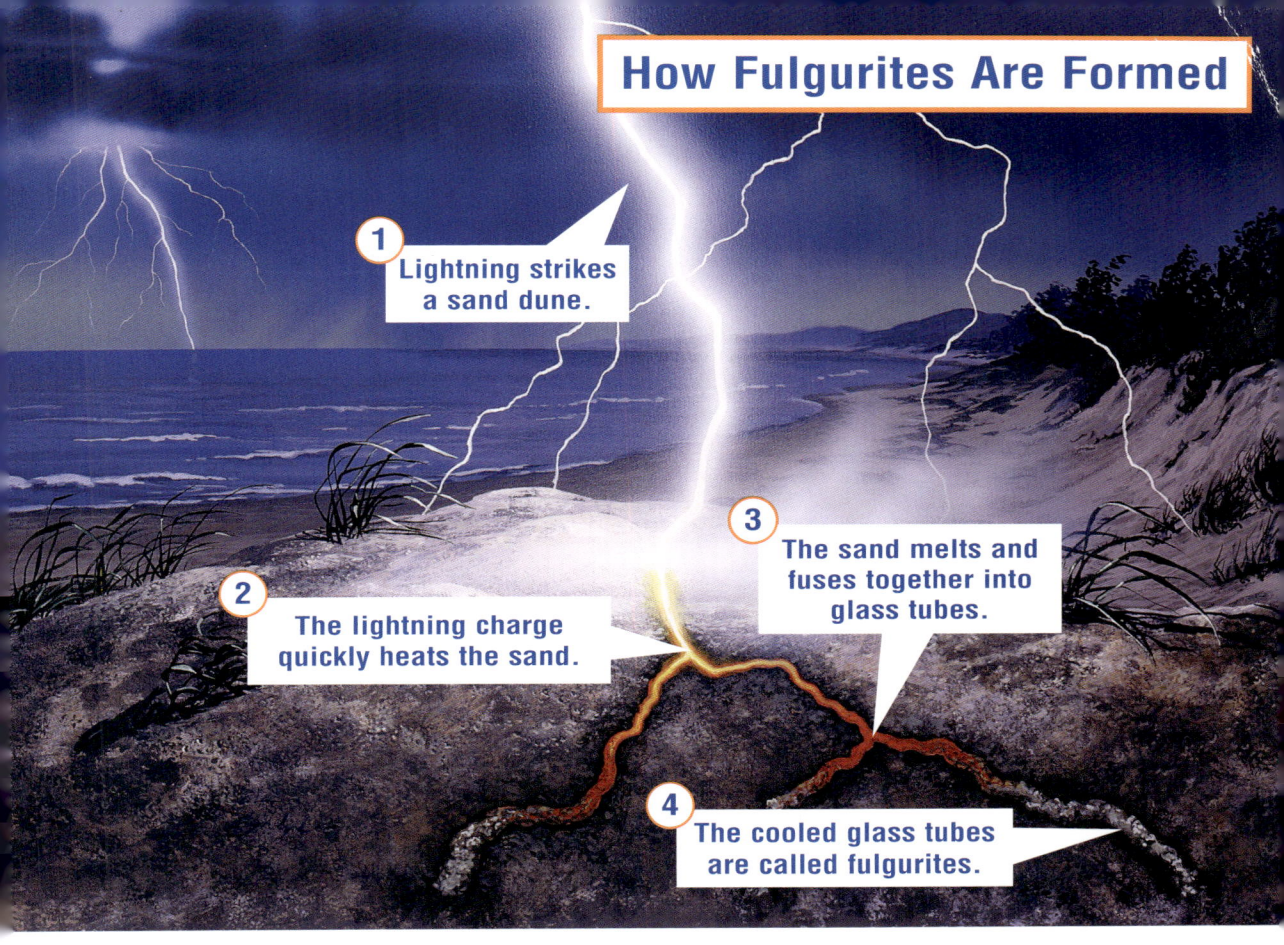

How Fulgurites Are Formed

1 Lightning strikes a sand dune.

2 The lightning charge quickly heats the sand.

3 The sand melts and fuses together into glass tubes.

4 The cooled glass tubes are called fulgurites.

common for lightning to strike dunes. When that happens, temperatures at the point of the strike can exceed fifty thousand degrees Fahrenheit—which is five times hotter than the surface of the sun. The tremendous amount of heat and energy created by a lightning strike can cause grains of sand to melt and then become solid again. This results in the formation of **fulgurites**, or hollow tubes of natural glass that are sometimes called fossilized lightning. Fulgurites resemble the roots of a tree, and their color depends on the sand that melts to form them. Most are tan colored, but they can also be black, white, or clear. They are very fragile and are usually no more than a couple of inches long. However, much larger fulgurites have been discovered buried in the sand. A team of Florida researchers found a fulgurite that was an astounding seventeen feet long.

From Ridges to Stars

One particularly interesting feature of sand dunes is their many different sizes and shapes. The size of a dune is determined by the amount of available sand, and the shape depends on the direction and strength of the wind. One type is the **barchan dune**, which is shaped like a crescent. Barchans are formed by wind that blows at them from two different directions. For example, wind might blow from the east during the summer and from the west in the winter. **Linear dunes** are ridges of sand that are formed by winds blowing from only one direction. They are the most common dunes along coastlines. **Star dunes** have a unique starlike shape because the wind blows at them from many different directions. **Parabolic dunes** are U-shaped, and they exist where climates are humid enough to allow vegetation to grow. Their long curved arms are covered by grass and trees that anchor them in place. So when the wind blows toward them, the only sand that moves is in the center, where there is no vegetation to hold it down.

Bouncing, Creeping, and Slumping

Some dunes are called **active dunes** because they move freely and rapidly. The speed at which they travel depends not only on their vegetation but also on their size, their shape, and the strength and direction of the wind. There are dunes that move only about a foot per year, and others that move much faster. Barchans, for instance, often move as much as eighty feet per year, but the more stable parabolic dunes barely move at all.

Most sand is moved by **saltation**, a process by which grains of sand skip and bounce along in the wind. As the sand collides with other grains, it forces them to move along the surface. This is known as **surface creep**. The sand piles up on the **windward** side of the dune and eventually works its way up to the crest. When the dune becomes top-heavy, sand tumbles down the steeply sloped **leeward** (back) side or **slip face**. Sometimes it trickles down slowly. Many times, though, **slumping** occurs, which is the collapse of a huge mass of sand. This continuous process of saltation and slumping causes dunes to move in the direction the wind

Parabolic dunes have a distinctive U shape. They exist only where the climate is humid enough to support the growth of vegetation.

blows. Over time, they are able to inch their way along the surface of the earth.

Whistles, Squeaks, and Booms

Just as intriguing as how dunes change and move are the various sounds they make. People describe the sounds in many different ways. Some hear singing noises, but others claim to hear whistling, barking, or squeaking. These sounds are caused by the grains of sand rubbing against each other.

Desert dunes are especially mysterious because of their booming sounds. Scientists believe these sounds are caused when grains of sand collide, such as when slumping occurs. In his book about sand dunes, author R.A. Bagnold describes one visit to the dunes of southwestern Egypt:

> On two occasions it happened on a still night, suddenly—a vibrant booming so loud that I had to shout to be heard by my companion. Soon other sources, set going by the disturbance, joined their music to the first, with so close a note that a slow beat was clearly recognized. This weird chorus went on for more than five minutes continuously before silence returned and the ground ceased to tremble. [1]

Sand dunes are nature's sand castles, molded and shaped by wind, sand, and time. Throughout the centuries, some have grown to be enormous, but others are still young and small. Some are constantly moving, but others are anchored in place by trees and grass. Sand dunes may share similar characteristics, but every one is its own unique and original sculpted work of art. There is, however, one way in which all dunes are the same: They are truly wonders of nature.

Wondrous Dunes

There is a vast difference between the dunes that rim the shores of America's Great Lakes and those found in the world's deserts. That is because the climates of the Great Lakes states are much cooler than those of desert areas. They are also more humid and receive large amounts of rainfall. These coastal dunes are often covered with grass and trees, which help to stabilize them by protecting them from the wind.

Sand dunes found throughout the world come in many different types and sizes. No one knows for sure where the smallest dunes are because they form and change so often. Large dunes, however, are much easier for scientists to identify. Some of the most enormous dunes on Earth are found throughout Africa, as well as in the countries of Peru and China. According to the United States Geological Survey, the star-shaped dunes of China's Badain Jaran Desert are up to sixteen hundred feet tall and are likely the tallest dunes on Earth. But Earth is not the only place where dunes are found. Robot spacecrafts launched by

China's sand dunes are some of the tallest in the world, with star-shaped formations reaching as high as sixteen hundred feet.

the National Aeronautic and Space Administration (NASA) have photographed many dunes on the planet Mars. NASA says that some of these dunes are very unique because they resemble sharks' teeth or chocolates.

Wondrous Dunes of the Desert

Deserts are found in many parts of the world, and desert dunes are a product of an extremely hot, dry climate where rainfall is rare. As a result, these dunes often have sparse vegetation or none at all. Also, fierce sandstorms are common in desert dunes. Author Janice Emily Bowers describes a morning in the Kelso Dunes in California's Mojave Desert: "With every step, clouds of sand swirled away from our feet. Sand beat against our flapping blue jeans, stung our bare hands and faces. A river of sand flowed around our ankles. Sand banners unfurled from the peaks and ridges of the highest dunes. The whole dune field was alive with rushing sand, a world in motion."[2]

Eight thousand miles from California, on the continent of Africa, is another desert that is famous for its dunes. The

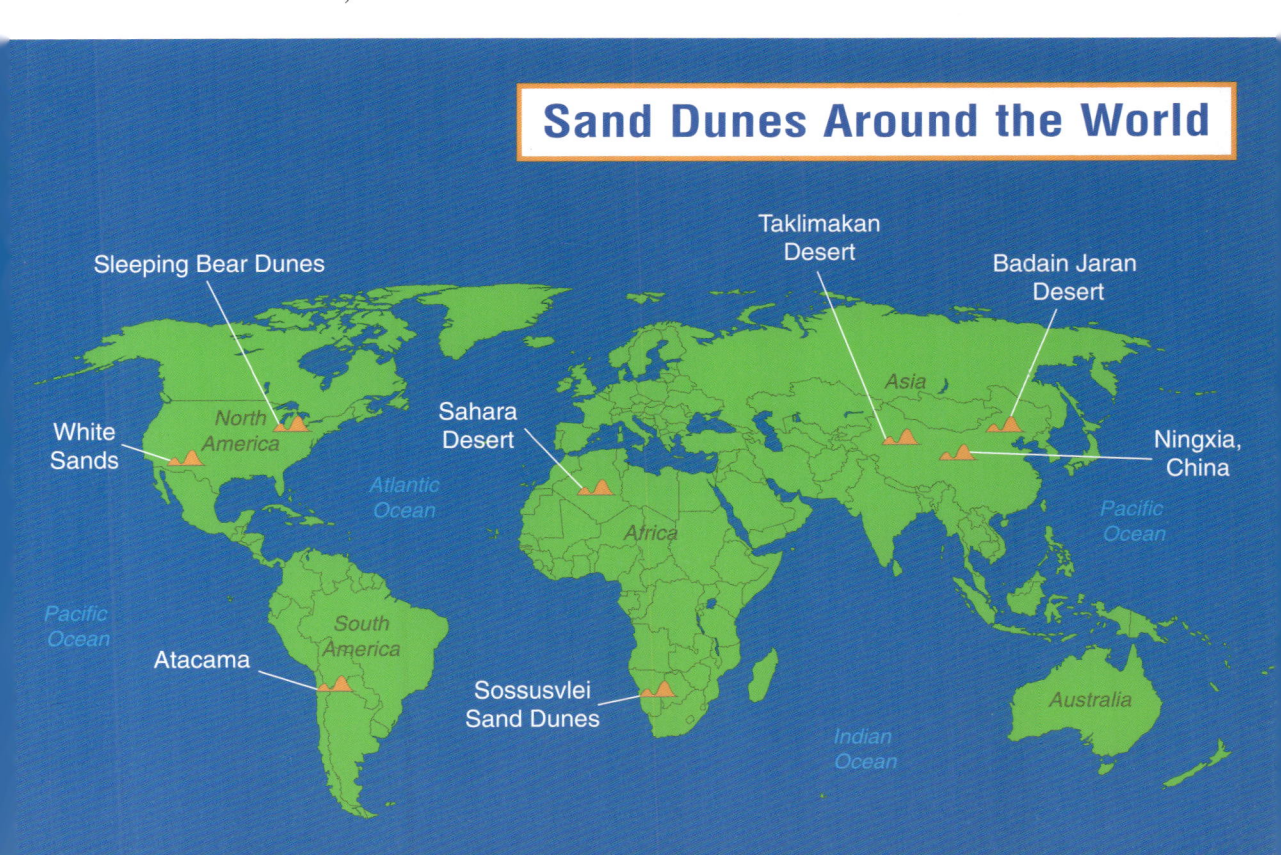

Sand Dunes Around the World

Namib Desert, located in the country of Namibia, is the oldest desert on Earth. It borders the coast of the Atlantic Ocean, and towering within it are the majestic dunes of Sossusvlei (pronounced "Shlu-shlu-way"). These are considered to be among the most awe-inspiring dunes in the world. One reason is that they are ancient: Geologists believe they are nearly 40 million years old. Also, the dunes are an unusual color. Because of their age, there is a high percentage of iron oxide in their sand. This causes the Sossusvlei dunes to vary from shades of apricot to burnt orange to deep, rich red. As strong desert winds blow, a shower of red sand billows off the dunes' crest, making them appear to be on fire.

Crazy Dune

The most spectacular of all the Sossusvlei dunes is "Big Daddy," one of the oldest and tallest dunes in the world. Big Daddy is nearly twelve hundred feet high—which is taller than a hundred-story building. The dune is so enormous that many visitors to Sossusvlei have the urge to climb it. People who live in nearby towns think the climbers are crazy, so their nickname for Big Daddy is "Crazy Dune."

James M. Clash, a writer who visited Namibia, was "crazy" enough to climb Big Daddy. He describes the experience: "The view from the top is not unlike that of the moon or Mars. For miles in all directions, hundreds of red dunes—all lesser in height, but impressive

A sand surfer glides down an African sand dune. The African continent is home to some of the oldest and tallest dunes in the world.

nonetheless—fill the horizon. Pitch-black shadows, combined with varying shades of bright red, give the scene a quality of surrealism [like a dream]."[3] Clash climbed the slip face of the dune, which was extremely steep. He says he had to crawl on all fours, like a giant spider, using his hands to anchor him so he would not keep sliding down.

Great Lakes Dunes

The dunes along America's "freshwater seas" are nothing like those found in the world's deserts. That is because the climates of Great Lakes states are much cooler than those of desert areas. They are also more humid and receive large amounts of rainfall. So these coastal dunes are often covered with grass and trees, which helps to stabilize them by protecting them from the wind. Yet even though these dunes are very different from desert dunes, they are every bit as fascinating.

Lake Michigan's coastline is bordered by the largest collection of freshwater dunes in the world. Dunes stretch for hundreds of miles along the coast, from the Indiana border northward to the Straits of Mackinac. Smaller numbers of dunes are also found along the coastlines of Lake Huron, Lake Superior, Lake Ontario, and Lake Erie.

Although Michigan's dunes are young compared to those in the Namib Desert, their formation began many thousands of years ago. During the **Ice Age**, when more than one-third of the earth was frozen, the area that is now Michigan was covered with thick ice sheets. There were also enormous masses of ice and rock debris called **glaciers**. The glaciers moved along the earth a few thousand feet per year, gouging and crushing rocks and anything else that lay in their path. Then, about ten thousand years ago, the climate grew warmer and the ice began to melt. Gradually the glaciers began to retreat, leaving behind giant heaps of rock known as **glacial moraines**.

The glaciers had also carved out huge basins in the earth that filled with water from the melting ice. These became known as the Great Lakes. Over time, the waves of the lakes pounded at the moraines and wore them down. This motion of water against rock created sand, which was carried deep into the lake bottoms. As the waves rolled in, they washed the sand back onto the shore. The wind blew, drying out the sand and piling it into drifts. The majestic Great Lakes dunes were born.

Namibia's colorful Sossusvlei dunes are located in the world's oldest desert and are believed to be more than 40 million years old.

The Sleeping Bear

The glacial moraines became the high bluffs that now overlook the Great Lakes. In some areas dunes formed on top of the bluffs, and these are called **perched dunes**. One of the most famous perched dune systems is Sleeping Bear National Lakeshore, which is located on the northern coast of Michigan's Lower Peninsula. The entire dune system stretches for thirty-five miles along Lake Michigan. Sleeping Bear, which is the largest of the dunes, rises 450 feet above the lake.

No one knows for sure how the dune got its name. But according to an old Indian story called the Legend of Sleeping Bear, it happened like this: Many years ago a mother bear and her two cubs escaped from a raging fire in the land that is now Wisconsin. They splashed into the rough waters

Grasses that grow on the dunes of the Great Lakes stabilize the dunes by protecting them from the wind.

According to Indian legend, a spirit formed the Manitou Islands on Lake Michigan to mark the place where two bear cubs drowned.

of Lake Michigan and swam for many hours. The mother encouraged the cubs to keep up, but they became tired and lagged behind. Nighttime came, and in the darkness the mother could no longer see the cubs. When she finally reached the shore, she expected them to be behind her. However, they were not there. Refusing to give up hope, the mother bear lay down to wait and soon fell asleep. As days, months, and seasons passed by, she stayed there by the shore, patiently waiting for her cubs. The wind blew and sand drifted over her until she was completely covered, forming a dune called Sleeping Bear. Later, to honor her for her loyalty, the Indian spirit Manitou created two islands in Lake Michigan. They were located in the place where the cubs had gone under the water. Today they are called South and North Manitou Islands.

The Sands of Time

The dunes of Sossusvlei and those gracing the Great Lakes shoreline are radically different from each other. Their climates are nothing alike, their sand color is different, and they are separated by thousands of miles and millions of years. Yet they are each unique in their own way—and as fascinating as they are famous.

CHAPTER THREE

Life in the Dunes

Sand dunes are far from lifeless places. Actually, some of the most beautiful, and most rare, varieties of plants and wildlife are found in the world's dune systems. These species are unique because over time they have adapted to their surroundings. Some live and flourish in cooler, more humid climates where water is plentiful. Others, however, manage to survive in conditions so harsh that any life at all seems miraculous.

Plants that live in desert dunes must withstand extremely hot and dry climates. They must also cope with constantly blowing sand. During sandstorms, drifts of sand can quickly bury grass and shrubs. To survive, plants must be able to grow faster than the sand can pile up around them. This is possible because of **photosynthesis**, the process by which plants make their own food. The most hardy desert dune plants are able to make their food more quickly than other vegetation, so they can grow faster. They also put down strong roots that anchor them and

Plants that live in dunes grow strong roots to secure them in place as the dunes shift with the wind.

keep them in place. So when the dunes move away from them, the plants will not simply blow away in the wind.

Survival of the Fittest

One place where conditions are especially harsh is in the dunes of the Namib Desert. During much of the year the climate is scorching hot, and sand temperatures can reach 130 degrees. Also, the dunes receive little or no rain— sometimes less than half an inch per year. Because of this harsh environment, few plants can survive in the Sossusvlei dunes. One type of vegetation that does grow is a type of golden dune grass. Another is a flowering plant called *Trianthema hereroensis*. This plant is rare and unique because it can survive for years without water. In the absence of rain, the plant makes use of the morning fog that rolls over the dunes from the nearby Atlantic. Its leaves, which are filled with empty spaces, absorb droplets of fog, storing the moisture to make it available for the plant's roots.

The heat and dryness in the Sossusvlei region also present a difficult environment for wildlife. Yet creatures do roam the dunes, including a variety of rodents, insects, and reptiles. Some of these are extremely rare. For example, the web-footed gecko lives nowhere else in the world but the Namib Desert. During the day, when the sand is at its hottest, the lizard stays burrowed underground. As soon as evening comes and temperatures begin to cool, it comes out to hunt for insects.

Another unusual reptile living in the Sossusvlei dunes is the shovel-snouted lizard. It is an amusing creature because

When the sands of the Sossusvlei dunes become too hot, the shovel-snouted lizard stands on only two feet at a time.

Animals of the Dunes

Lizard

Oryx

Sidewinder

Beetle

Camel

Whitefronted Plover

Gecko

it "dances" when the sand becomes too hot for its feet. Using its tail for balance, the lizard stands on only two feet at a time. When those feet get hot, it hops to the other pair. Sometimes even the dancing fails to keep it cool enough, so the lizard dives into the sand and burrows down to where it is cooler.

A rare mammal that lives in the Sossusvlei dunes is the oryx, a member of the antelope family. The oryx, which is about the size of a stocky pony, is white and either black or brown with sharp V-shaped horns and a long black tail. These animals adapt well to the harshest desert climates because they can go for months without any water. All the water they need comes from the vegetation they eat, such as the moisture-filled tsama melons that grow throughout the Namib Desert. Also, the oryx can cope with extreme heat and dryness by raising its body temperature as high as 116 degrees (an average human's body temperature is 98.6 degrees). This prevents it from perspiring, so more water is retained in its body.

Life in the Snow-White Sands

The conditions in North America's desert dunes are not as harsh as those of Namibia. Still, the climates are very hot and dry. For instance, temperatures in New Mexico's White Sands dunes can exceed a hundred degrees during the summer months. Plus, the area receives only about eight inches of rain per year. Most of the rain falls during the winter months. When the rains come, wildflowers such as pink sand verbena and white dune evening primrose begin to bloom. For a few months, the dunes are alive with color and sweet fragrance.

During the spring, though, the environment radically changes in the White Sands dunes. Winds can gust up to forty-five miles per hour, causing fierce sandstorms. The blowing sand creates an environment in which only the hardiest plants can survive. One such plant is the soaptree yucca, a palmlike shrub with long bell-shaped white flowers. This plant grows very fast, as much as one foot per year. It is a particularly unusual species because it seems to sense when faster-than-normal growth is necessary. When sand starts piling up around it, the plant's stem begins to grow rapidly, pushing the green leafy part above the surface of the sand. The soaptree yucca appears to be only three or four feet tall. However, with its long roots it may actually be thirty or forty feet tall—sometimes as tall as the dune itself.

Like the oryx that roams Namibia's dunes, creatures that live in White Sands must get most of the water they need from the food they eat. For example, the kangaroo rat, a rodent that resembles a small kangaroo, eats only dry seeds and does not drink water. It can survive because it makes its own water inside its body while digesting food. To preserve moisture, the kangaroo rat does not perspire. During the heat of the day, when it is burrowed deep in the ground, the animal seals the entrance to its den. This helps keep the heat out and the moisture in.

Two other creatures that live in the White Sands dunes are the Apache pocket mouse and the bleached earless lizard. Both creatures are as white as the dunes in which they live. This keeps them cool by reflecting the rays of

In the White Sands dunes the soaptree yucca (pictured) grows long, strong roots to anchor itself into the soil.

the sun. Their pale color also helps them blend in with the sand, so they are not easily seen by predators.

The Flora of Freshwater Dunes

The plants and wildlife living in the dunes of the Great Lakes do not have to work nearly as hard to survive. Yet they still endure a challenging environment. Even though climates are much cooler than those of desert areas, sand temperatures can be more than a hundred degrees in the summer. The winter months are the harshest of all, with frigid temperatures, killing frost, and severe ice storms. The plants that survive in these dunes must be able to cope with drastic changes in weather.

Plants that grow on the sand dunes of the Great Lakes are hardy enough to survive both the scorching heat of summer and the freezing cold of winter.

Marram grass is a form of dune grass that thrives in the Great Lakes dunes. It has a waxy coating that helps protect it from the abrasive blowing sand. However, its ability to survive under harsh conditions is mostly due to an elaborate root system. Much like the soaptree yucca, drifting sand actually stimulates the marram grass to grow rapidly. As sand piles up around it, the plant's strong underground stems send new shoots to the surface. This enables the grass to grow taller, so its bladelike leaves stay above the sand and remain exposed to the sun. More sand piles up, and more marram grass shoots up through the sand. Because of this ongoing process, marram grass plays an important part in helping the Great Lakes dunes grow taller. It also stabilizes the dunes by trapping sand, keeping it from blowing away.

The Great Lakes dunes are also home to other plants and wildflowers, including several types of orchids. In addition, there are numerous varieties of trees. Many of the dunes near the Great Lakes coastline are covered with lush forests of jack pines, oaks, and hickories.

The plants and creatures that live in the world's dunes are as different as the dunes themselves. Some must cope with soaring temperatures and make do with what little moisture they can extract from fog. Others endure fierce sandstorms, blazing hot sand, or cold, harsh winters. Yet in spite of their constant struggle to survive, these species manage to adapt to their environments. Their very presence is one more reason why sand dunes are miracles of nature.

CHAPTER FOUR

Swallowed by Dunes!

Dunes are indeed intriguing and beautiful, but they can also be menacing. It takes a long time, but because of the way dunes creep across the earth, they can eventually fill in lakes and rivers. They can even bury entire cities and towns. In some places dunes now dominate the landscape—and buried beneath them lay the ruins of a place where people once lived, worked, and played.

A Ghost Town

In southwestern Michigan there once was a town called Singapore. Founded in the 1830s by a man named Oshea Wilder, Singapore was located on the banks of the Kalamazoo River. Only large, tree-covered sand dunes separated the town from Lake Michigan.

Wilder's dream was that Singapore would eventually become a major lake port, much like Milwaukee and Chicago. People soon began to move to the town, and they built homes where they could raise their families. By

1870 Singapore had a bank, a general store, two hotels, a small school, and two sawmills. The town was growing rapidly. Then in 1871, when a disastrous fire destroyed much of Chicago, there was suddenly a great demand for lumber to rebuild the city. The Singapore sawmills became busier than they had ever been before.

It only took a few years to chop down the vast pine forests that grew throughout the county, including those covering the dunes. Once the trees were cut up in the sawmills, the wood was sold. Then it was loaded on a fleet

Egypt's Great Sphinx of Giza was buried beneath sand for centuries. Over time sand dunes can even bury entire towns.

of lumber schooners and was carried across Lake Michigan to Chicago. By 1875 the forests were gone and the land was bare, so there was no longer any need for Singapore's mills. The largest mill was loaded on a schooner and transported north to Point St. Ignace. One month later a neighboring town's newspaper read, "Nothing remains of a once thriving village but a few scattered houses, and hereafter Singapore must be considered among the things that were."[+]

The people of Singapore began to abandon the town. Some had their houses moved to Saugatuck, a village to the south. Most, however, just packed up their belongings

A house in Pacific City, Oregon, is buried by moving sand dunes.

and left. Soon, with no trees to cover and protect the dunes, strong winds off the lake began to blow the sand. Slowly the dunes crept toward Singapore, and by the turn of the century the town was completely buried. A historical sign, which now stands in front of the Saugatuck city hall, reads, "Beneath the sands near the mouth of the Kalamazoo River lies the site of Singapore, one of Michigan's most famous ghost towns. . . . When the supply of timber was exhausted the mills closed, the once bustling waterfront grew quiet. . . . Gradually, Lake Michigan's shifting sands buried Singapore."

Buried Fishing Villages

Singapore is just one example of how dunes can move when trees and other vegetation are destroyed. The same thing has happened throughout history in many areas of the world. That is because in the past, people did not know that vegetation was needed to keep the dunes in place.

One region that was nearly lost because of moving sand dunes is a long strip of land called the Curonian Spit, which is located in the European country of Lithuania. The spit runs along the coastline of the Baltic Sea, and it is rimmed with sand dunes. People began to settle there several thousand years ago, when the dunes were covered with grass and trees. Most of the settlers made their living by fishing, although many were also farmers. The years went by and the population continued to grow. More land was needed to grow crops, so the trees were chopped down to create additional farmland. However, once the dunes had been stripped of their protective vegetation, they lay bare and vulnerable. Strong coastal winds began to pound the dunes, sending drifts of sand toward the villages. By the beginning of the nineteenth century, fourteen villages had been completely buried.

This did not have the same unfortunate ending as the story of Singapore, however. In 1803 a professor from a surviving village warned that the entire spit would be buried by sand. He proposed that trees and shrubs be planted on the dunes to stabilize them. He also had an unusual idea: that a new dune should be built by humans and then planted with trees. This, he believed, would further lessen the risk of the dunes taking over. The people were in favor of the professor's ideas. They worked together to plant trees and build the new dune. Because of their efforts, and the efforts of many other people over the years, the Curonian Spit did not suffer the same fate as the villages from the past. Today, instead of separate villages, there is one city called Neringa. It is a place known for its beautiful sand dunes—and for the lush green forests that protect them.

Menacing Dunes

In some parts of the world, the migration of sand dunes has not been stopped or even slowed. Instead, the dunes continue to creep toward cities and towns, growing more threatening each day. One country where the risk is especially great is China. In the northern part of the country, dunes are moving toward some villages at a rate of more than sixty-five feet per year. This is partly the result of a severe, prolonged drought—but humans are to blame as well. Many forests have been cut down and grasslands have been overgrazed by livestock, leaving the land bare of vegetation. This has resulted in **desertification**, or the expansion of the desert.

Sandstorms are frequent and fierce in northern China, and dunes now cover areas that were once fertile farmland. One village, called Longbaoshan, is gradually being swallowed by drifting sand. The people of the village have nowhere to go, and as the dunes move closer and closer, they can do nothing but wait and watch. One farmer expressed his concern: "The dune was way off over there. But just in the last few years, it has begun to move towards us, very quickly."[5] The Chinese government has started a

Sandstorms are frequent and fierce in northern China.

Trees planted in sand dunes help stabilize the dunes and prevent sand from blanketing neighboring villages.

major campaign to stop the destruction of forests. It has also demanded that the people help to plant thousands of trees. However, even government officials know these efforts are not enough. As the dunes threaten to overtake Chinese villages, towns, and farms, the country continues its desperate search for ways to stop them.

If They Could Only Talk

Sand dunes may be viewed as menacing or as awe-inspiring natural wonders. The reality is, they can be both. Dunes have been shaped by nature and by humans who have helped to shape them through their careless abuse of the land. If dunes could talk, perhaps they could clear up some of the mysteries that surround them. Exactly how did they form and when? What was the earth like then? How have they changed, and how will they look in the future? Where will they be a hundred years from now? Geologists who study dunes know some of these answers, but other answers remain unknown. And that, quite likely, is something that will never change.

Notes

Chapter One: Amazing Mountains of Sand

1. R.A. Bagnold, *The Physics of Blown Sand and Desert Dunes.* New York: William Morrow, 1965, p. 250.

Chapter Two: Wondrous Dunes

2. Janice Emily Bowers, *Dune Country.* Tucson: University of Arizona Press, 1986, p. 13.
3. James M. Clash, "Big Daddy: The Mother of All Dunes," Environmental News Network, August 24, 2000. www.enn.com.

Chapter Four: Swallowed by Dunes!

4. Quoted in Kit Lane, *Buried Singapore: Michigan's Imaginary Pompeii.* Douglas, MI: Pavilion, 1994, p. 44.
5. Quoted in Adam Brookes, "China Battles Against Sand Invasion," *BBC News,* June 6, 2000. http://news.bbc.co.uk.

Glossary

active dunes: Dunes that move more rapidly than other dunes.

barchan dune: A crescent-shaped dune.

desertification: The expansion of a desert into other land.

fulgurite: A hollow tube of natural glass created when sand is melted by lightning and then becomes solid again.

glacial moraine: A giant heap of rock left behind by retreating glaciers.

glacier: An enormous mass of ice and rock debris.

Ice Age: A time in history when more than one-third of the earth was covered with thick sheets of ice.

leeward: The steeply sloped back side of a dune.

linear dune: A ridge-shaped dune.

parabolic dune: A U-shaped dune with long curved arms that are covered by vegetation.

perched dune: A dune that sits on top of a glacial moraine.

photosynthesis: The process by which plants make their own food.

saltation: A process by which grains of sand skip and bounce along in the wind.

slip face: Another word for the leeward, or back, side of a dune.

slumping: The collapse of a huge mass of sand down the slip face of a dune.

star dune: A star-shaped dune whose shape is created by wind blowing from many different directions.

surface creep: Grains of sand that are pushed along the surface by other sand grains.

windward: The front side of a dune where sand piles up.

For Further Exploration

Books

Jan Gumprecht Bannan, *Sand Dunes*. Minneapolis, MN: Carolrhoda Books, 1990. This book primarily focuses on dunes along the coastline of Oregon, but it also covers several other Western Hemisphere dune systems. It explains the different types of dunes and how they were formed.

Madelyn Wood Carlisle, *Let's Investigate Soft, Shimmering Sand*. Hauppauge, NY: Barron's Educational Series, 1993. This book discusses what sand is and how it is formed. It also explains how beaches and dunes are built up and the types of animals and plants that survive in the desert.

Roy A. Gallant, *Sand on the Move: The Story of Dunes*. New York: Franklin Watts, 1997. This work discusses dune formation, types of sand, and different shapes of dunes as well as plants and wildlife that live in dune areas.

Mary Maruca, *A Kid's Guide to Exploring Great Sand Dunes National Monument and Preserve*. Tucson, AZ: Western National Parks Association, 2002. This is an informative book about Colorado's Great Sand Dunes, which are the tallest dunes in North America.

Periodicals

Tina Adler, "Blowing in the Wind," *National Geographic World*, June 1999. This article discusses how moving sand dunes can creep toward cities, towns, and farms, and eventually bury them.

Lyn Bourdow, "Shifting Sands/Buried Lightning," *Cricket*, November 2000. An informative article about Jockey's Ridge, a North Carolina sand dune system that is moving as much as six feet per year.

Beth Geiger, "Dune Tunes: What Makes Sand Dunes and Beaches Sing?" *Weekly Reader Current Science*, November 23, 2001. This article explores the mysterious phenomenon of "singing sand," one of the most intriguing characteristics of dune systems.

Internet Sources

Andrew Alden, "Here's Sand in Your Eye," About.com, October 5, 1997. http://geology.about.com/library/weekly/aa100597.htm. An interesting article that includes much information about sand dunes, including an explanation about sand. Also, there are links to photos of some famous dunes in China, as well as .wav files that play the "music" of the dunes.

Kids Cosmos, "Sand Dunes and Martian Winds," February 10, 2002. www.kidscosmos.org/kid-stuff/kids-sand.html. An interesting story about the types of sand dunes that scientists have discovered on Mars.

Rosemary Wilson, "Creeping Sand," NASA Kids, April 24, 2003. http://kids.msfc.nasa.gov. An interesting and informative article about how and why sand moves—on Mars as well as on Earth—and the effect this has on dunes.

Web site

White Sands National Monument Kids' Site (www.nps. gov/whsa/pphtml/kids.html). This site includes information and activities that can help kids learn about the geology, animals, and plants of New Mexico's White Sands National Monument.

Index

Picture Credits

Cover image: © Michele Westmoreland/CORBIS
© James L. Amos/CORBIS, 19
© Anthony Bannister; Gallo Images/CORBIS, 36
Chase Studio/Photo Researchers, Inc., 7
© Christie's Images/CORBIS, 31
Corel, 24 (images)
© Ric Ergenbright/CORBIS, 32
© Gallo Images/CORBIS, 23
Manfred Gottschalk/Lonely Planet Images, 17
© Catherine Karnow/CORBIS, 6
Paul Kennedy/Lonely Planet Images, 14
Mark Newman/Lonely Planet Images, 5
Carol Polich/Lonely Planet Images, 27
© James Randklev/CORBIS, 22
Keren Su/Lonely Planet Images, 12
© Ken Wagner/ Visuals Unlimited, 28
© Ed Wargin/CORBIS, 18
© Michael S. Yamashita/CORBIS, 35
© Bo Zaunders/CORBIS, 9

About the Author

Peggy J. Parks holds a bachelor of science degree from Aquinas College in Grand Rapids, Michigan, where she graduated magna cum laude. She is a freelance author who has written more than twenty-five books for Gale Group's KidHaven Press, Blackbirch Press, and Lucent Books. Parks lives in Muskegon, Michigan, a town she says inspires her writing because of its location on the shores of Lake Michigan.